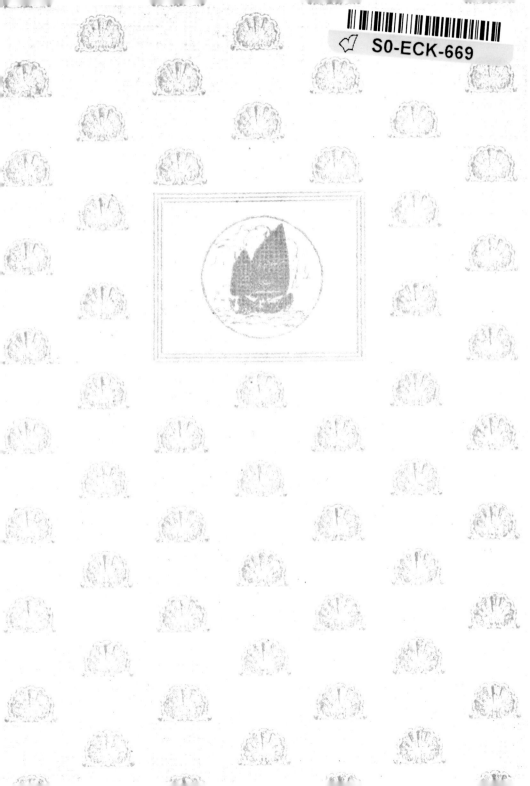

CHINESE JUNKS

AND OTHER NATIVE CRAFT

STERN—FOOCHOW POLE JUNK

CHINESE JUNKS

AND OTHER NATIVE CRAFT

BY

IVON·A·DONNELLY

GRAHAM BRASH, SINGAPORE

First published in 1924

This edition published in 1988 by
Graham Brash (Pte) Ltd
36-C Prinsep Street
Singapore 0718

ISBN 9971-49-097-8

Cover design by Teo Kim Heng
Printed in Singapore by
Hong Kong Offset Printing Pte Ltd

PREFATORY NOTE

OWING to the success of a small book of sketches of Chinese Junks published some four years ago, and in response to numerous requests for a larger and improved edition, I put this book before the public with the hope that it may prove to stimulate Western interest in the seacraft of the most ancient of civilizations.

In the descriptions of the various craft, which must needs be short, I have tried to avoid technicalities, and have only mentioned the more salient and interesting points connected with the craft under review. To the average Westerner the term "junk" conjures up visions of a strange unseaworthy vessel with big eyes, totally unfit to carry man and his commerce across the high seas, but I hope that the introduction and the brief descriptions of the various types, together with the illustrations given, will dispel this idea which is entirely erroneous.

To those friends who have so kindly lent me their assistance, and through whose encouragement and help this edition of "CHINESE JUNKS" has been made possible, my sincerest thanks are due. If the readers of this book have been converted to a new view of Chinese water craft and have derived half the pleasure that I have had in writing it, then I am amply repaid for the time spent.

I. A. DONNELLY

Tientsin, North China,
September, 1924.

TABLE OF CONTENTS

LIST OF ILLUSTRATIONS

CHINESE JUNKS
AND OTHER NATIVE CRAFT

INTRODUCTORY

ALTHOUGH much has been written on China and her people, very little has been said about one of her most important industries — shipping. And this, notwithstanding the fact that China has been from the earliest times one of the foremost amongst sea-faring nations. This omission is surprising when one remembers that there are more vessels in China than in all the rest of the world put together.

Brief reference to Chinese craft has been made in all the standard works, *i.e.*, "*Torr's Ancient Ships*," "*Sailing Ships and their Story*," etc., etc., but particulars in regard to the number, variety and style have been insignificant; also in the majority of cases such pictures and models as are available have been grossly exaggerated.

WARRINGTON SMITH has dealt with Chinese junks in his "*Mast and Sail*," and his sketches of *Southern China Fishers* and some of the Coasters are delightful, but he has only written of those met with in the regular steamer tracks. MAJOR LORING'S book of Hongkong types also shows something of the South China variety.

It must be borne in mind that every port, every inlet and lake has its own peculiar vessel best suited to its particular waters, currents and needs. Literally their name is legion. It would, therefore, be a brave man who would venture to describe in detail all the junks in use by the Chinese. Week ends spent on the Whangpoo, journeys on the great Yangtsze and elsewhere, up and down the coast, and in the interior give the writer confidence that of the thousands of junks offered to the observant eye, at least a representative number of types are shown.

Several writers in the past have adversely criticised the Chinese junk. It has been said to be slow and unwieldy, and absolutely unfit as a sea boat. Because John Chinaman is essentially industrious, a money-seeker, and always content with a "bird in the hand" it has been put down to his natural vanity that he has not learnt to copy the fine ships of the west which visit his coasts. The writer emphatically disagrees with these opinions. No nation has shewn greater independence in arts and craft than the Chinese. The originality that pervades their architecture, painting and whole life ashore and afloat has no comparison in the world. That their manners, modes and methods appear upside down, and contrary to all Western ideas and thoughts does not prove that there is no good in them — and even so with their ships.

Actually in this respect they have little to learn from the Western hemisphere. Western Nations on the other hand have learnt and copied a great deal from the Chinese. A case in point is the system of watertight compartments. Although we have no historical records of the date when the Chinese first originated this idea, we know that it was many centuries before Father le Comte, writing on Chinese craft in 1687 (*Ref. "Collections of Voyages and Travels*," Vol. 2, page 510), stated :—

> "Their barks are made of a very fine light timber, which makes them more apt to take all impressions one has a mind to

give them. They divide into five or six compartments, so that if they touch upon a point of rock which makes a break in their vessel, only one part of the boat is filled, and the others are dry, and defend them until they can mend the hole in the other."

Many decades before the turret principle for the saving of tonnage dues was evolved in Europe the great Pechili traders from North China, big five-masted, three to four hundred ton vessels, sailed the high seas.

The leeboards now so common in the shallow type of boats on the English and Dutch coasts were in use in China many centuries before the seafarers of Europe became aware of their value.

Although considerable controversy has raged over the origin of the compass we have it from Chinese records that Chow-kung-taoche-man-chay (The Duke of Chow) first made the compass about A.D. 1112. There are no records in Europe to disprove this fact and it is merely conjecture on which the historians of the West pin their faith.

The writers who treat the Chinese junk with scorn and contempt are invariably "landlubbers." They have not studied the junk at sea, in harbour, and at work; nor the sailorman himself and his prowess as a seafarer and navigator. One can see it in the illustrations given us from time to time in glowing caricature.

In comparatively recent years the Chinese junk has proved its capability for undertaking long sea voyages (see "Foochow Pole Junks," and "Amoy Fishing Junk," pages 97 and 107).

It is not surprising that the Chinese with such a large population directly interested in water transport by sea, canal, creek and river, should prove to be wonderful sailors. A big proportion of China's teeming millions have their home on the water. They are born on junks, grow up, live and die on junks. During this process from birth to old age there is nothing they have not learnt about the vessel to which they are rooted, neither, being an observant people, does much escape them in the study of the winds and waves which are life or death to their floating homes. In this connection it may be of interest to note here that in and around Hongkong there are no less than 69,000 "tan-ka" or sampan folk having their homes on the innumerable craft plying in and out of the harbour.

The Chinese sailorman has been called the Dutchman of the East owing to his similar habit of making his boat his home. Also there is a great similarity in his tastes as regards ships. He has the same love of bluff lines, bright colours and varnish, long pole masts with vanes and the same brown coloured sails, while both countries are countries of rivers and canals.

On the larger Chinese vessels the family living on board have what they would consider quite comfortable quarters in the lofty poop, although no doubt a European would expire from the foetid atmosphere and general "smelliness." To a Chinaman these details are not noticeable. Invariably the vessel is overcrowded, old men, young men, women and children, all jumbled up together, eating, drinking, playing, smoking, and of course gambling, in its nooks on deck, or its depths below. For months and years, at sea, in port, in typhoon and calm, they live quite happily in this way. In the present day, however, women are not often seen on ocean-going junks.

Perhaps one of the greatest characteristics of the Chinese sailorman is his adaptability. His training is such that literally he can handle the most unlikely vessel in a masterly manner under almost any conditions. It is no surprise, therefore, to find that given a really fine specimen of his native junk he is an artist in his manipulations of her.

Like all seafarers the Chinese junkman is a superstitious soul. Everything in connection with his expeditions is governed by the gods, therefore it is necessary that much propitiation is made to them, or in the words of the laodah "must wanchee pay plenty chin chin joss." The date of departure is always governed by "Feng-shui," a curious Chinese custom which is supposed to be the influence of the wind and water spirits for good or ill.

The first act of homage at the outset of a voyage belongs to the joss of the compass, which in China is a primitive affair of 24 points. The idea is that the "Powers that be" send fine weather and favourable winds. Should the reverse happen, there is undoubtedly a "Jonah" on board who must be removed at the next port.

At night when a fleet of fishing boats "go about" they light flares and beat gongs to frighten away the devils of the sea. Doubtless this habit also tends towards avoiding collision, for there is always a certain amount of practical sense in the Chinaman's ideas, even in his "joss" pidgin. This beating of gongs is also a ceremony that takes place on the departure on a voyage of one junk from its fellows at a crowded anchorage.

Every junk carries its own particular little "joss" idol on the poop. Much burning of silver joss paper representing "sycee" (money in the form of a silver shoe) takes place before him. Certainly the Chinaman's faith is childlike and great—if bad weather is met with an extra supply of joss paper is burnt, and on safe arrival at the journey's end thanksgiving is made, accompanied by the beating of gongs.

The "eye" painted on the bows of so many junks is a superstition generally attributed to the Chinese, the theory being that to a Chinaman a junk is a fish, which without any eye could not see how to go on its way. The writer is inclined to believe that this is one of those customs that the Chinese copied from the Arabs who followed the old Egyptian habit of placing the eye of Osiris on the prow of a vessel. This idea is confirmed by the fact that the "eye" is never made use of by inland craft nor is it found on the older type of Chinese seagoing craft — such as the Pechili Trader and the Antung Trader — but only on the junks hailing from ports which from the earliest days have been Arab centres of trade. A case in point is the junk hailing from Ta-pu-to the port for Kiaochow which was an important Arab settlement in the fourth century. The hull generally is exactly the same as the Pechili Trader but the vessel makes use of the eye, whereas the similar vessels from the more Northern ports do not.

Having described the sailorman and his habits let us now take the hull generally. These can be divided into two classes. Those with bluff bows and lines, and those finely moulded and sharp ended. In the Northern types — practically the oldest Chinese type in existence — we see a swim-headed vessel with flat bottom. They are built in this manner on account of the ports to which they trade being invariably up a river full of shallows and sand banks. South of the Yangtsze Cape we find a rock bound coast with deep harbours accessible to vessels of any draft. Here are finely moulded deep sea craft with lines which compare favourably with any of our finest racing yachts.

The bow of a junk is one of its distinctive features. In the northern and river types this is usually box shaped, but in the Southern types of sea going craft it is open with two wings or cheeks on either side between which a transverse beam is fitted on which the anchor windlass is fitted. Here too, may be seen the great single fluke wooden anchors with shanks twelve or more feet in length, and weighted very often with stones. Four fluke iron anchors are also used. Of course the arrangement differs in each type of boat, but the general idea is the same. The Swatow and Hongkong types, however, do not affect the wings as they are flush decked vessels with no bulwarks.

Every junk is divided into watertight compartments. This subdivision of the hull besides being for the safety of the ship has also other advantages inasmuch as it is carried out to such an extent that ribs are not used at all. In common with most things Chinese which appear to the Westerner as "topsy turvy" it is interesting to note that in a large number of cases the beams and knees forming the framework of a junk are placed on top, thus giving the acme of comfort inside with no nasty projecting beams on which to knock one's head below. Incidentally there is more stowage room for the cargo.

The wetted surface of a junk is reduced almost to the theoretical minimum in comparison with its displacement. The sheer line of the bottom illustrates a peculiarity — the run is carried out quite full, almost to the stern, and then comes up with a sharp turn. This, however, does not seem to affect its speed in any way. There is always a marked flat portion on the bottom of the hull, so that the vessel can go aground and rest at low tide without heeling over. Even the sharp ended Southern types are built in this manner, and time and time again, one will see a junk high and dry on the banks of a river or on the coast being painted, caulked or repaired. There is no need for a dock for overhaul, anywhere will do.

The masts are invariably stepped between partners which extend about half the width of the mast again. These partners are not parallel but narrow down towards the bottom while the heel of the mast is cut down slightly so as to form a wedge and the mast is jambed between them into the step. Occasionally, however, toggle pins are made use of in the smaller craft so that the mast can be lowered when required. On either side of the tabernable in which the mast is stepped a windlass is fitted which is used for hauling up the heavy battened sails. In the big Foochow pole junks, lorchas, and some of the Northern traders, the modern type of hand capstan is used.

Aft of the foremast, and just for'ard of the mainmast, a "horse" is stepped on which the heavy sails fall when lowered. In the case of the larger junks where the mainsail does not rest on the deck of the house aft another is fitted at the break of the poop.

The stern is always higher than the bow as it was in all our ships of bygone days. Modern practice in the West has changed all this, but here again, John Chinaman feels he knows best, and in this the writer thinks he is correct, especially for the work he has to do around the coast. The vessel will more easily lie head to wind in a gale, and moreover stands a better chance against being "pooped" by an overtaking wave in a heavy sea. Also from his point of vantage on the high poop where he works the unwieldy tiller, the steersman commands a good view over the bow of the boat. In the smaller type of fishing craft there is no planking at the stern of the boat above the level of the deck. The reason for this would appear to be that in a following sea, when a wave hits the vessel, a planked up stern would tend, with the open stern, to make her bury her head, whereas a large quantity of water is taken aboard temporarily in the well and acts as ballast; this not only keeps her head up but prevents the stern from lifting unduly. The moment the sea has passed the water runs out again through the scuppers or over the side amidships.

In all Chinese vessels the crew's quarters will be found aft. In the larger vessels in the deck house on the poop, and in the smaller types under deck aft.

The frequent absence of a keel in a junk is against good work to windward, but the deep rudder, which at sea is lowered down the trunk and extends well below the ship, helps considerably to hold the vessel up to the wind. The forefoot and gripe (which only appear in the Hongkong and Swatow types) which is often extended under the bows is also of considerable assistance in this respect. It may be of interest to mention here that some of the smaller sampans resort to a dagger board for windward work.

The Chinese sail is a balanced lug, extended and stiffened by battens, and usually made of cotton cloth or matting. In the sudden squalls and typhoons which are numerous about the coasts at certain seasons of the year this is the type most easily handled. In case of emergency no reefing is needed, the halyard is let go, and the weight of the sails and battens bring the sails down into the topping lifts. It is therefore made snug quite speedily. Invariably the Chinese junk, especially the seagoing type, has three masts or more, a fore, main and mizzen, with perhaps a jigger or two and in common with other blue water sailors the Chinaman appreciates the advantage of splitting up his sail area into component parts for greater facility in handling. This system of course is much more convenient for bringing a vessel into stays or paying her off when tacking. The five masted Pechili traders are a case in point.

The luff of the sail is cut in various ways. In the North like the leech it is straight up and down the mast. In the middle types there is not much difference but in the Hongkong cargo boats and the West River craft it stands out well before the mast bringing the centre of effort well forward. The Chinaman uses no jib, but steps his foremast well up in the eyes raking over the bows and sets a large foresail on it in the shape of another lug.

The sail is hoisted on a pole mast—often a very fine spar. The halyard passes through a large double block on the yard, and a treble block on the mast head. On the Antung and Northern types there is no block and the halyards are run through sheaves at the top of the mast. A hauling parrel to the yard keeps it to the mast and helps to peak the sail when reefed. Each batten has its own parrel and its own single part leading to the main sheet.

Sometimes on the bigger craft in lighter winds a main staysail is set between the fore and main mast and a flying topmast staysail aloft; the smaller vessels make use of innumerable types of spinnakers. In the river craft plying up and down the small creeks and rivers the mainsail is a very high affair, and from outward appearances these craft would appear to be very much over canvassed. These high sails, however, are absolutely necessary to catch the breezes over the tops of the banks.

In the opinion of some yachtsmen the high square leeched sail of the river craft plying on the Whangpoo river is one of the most mathematically correct rigs, being very similar, when filled, to the wing of an aeroplane. It is said that these vessels sail about as close to the wind as it is possible for any boat to. This is probably due to the multiple sheets which enable the peak to be hauled in and lie fair with the heel of the sail, unlike the Western type in which the peak when sailing close hauled is inclined to fall away and flap.

In these heavy sails there is a tendency for the whole sail to swing forward so the fore end of each batten of the sail is brought aft to the mast by a lacing which can be hauled on or slackened up as may be required from the deck. By this means the battens can be towsed aft and the required peak given to the sail while the friction and strain are distributed evenly over the whole mast. The moment the halyard is slacked off everything else slackens automatically and is never likely to jam in a squall.

A feature that strikes one about the rigging of a Chinese junk is that the heavy masts carry no stays whatsoever. Gybing is thus simplicity itself. When this manœuvre is seen performed the first time the yachtsman from the West fully expects to see the masts lifted right out of the boat as the heavy yard swings across with a rattle and crash. It is very seldom, however, one sees a junk dismasted in this manner and it would seem that the secret lies entirely in the even distribution of the weight all up and down the mast. A spritsail is very often used on the smaller type of fishing craft working off the Yangtsze Cape, and on some of the river craft near and around Shanghai.

It is a noticeable feature in the pole junks that the mast, a very heavy spar made of iron wood, is built up with heavy stiffeners bound round with iron bands. The bamboo hawser which is one of the most important parts of a junk's equipment is also one of those entirely Chinese products that cannot fail to interest the stranger, and convince him of the ingenuity of the Chinese for making use of this useful tree.

Having written of the junk herself, the crew sails, rigging etc., we will now turn to that part of her — the picturesque — that so appeals to the artist. We have said that John China-man, like the Dutchman, likes bright varnish and colours. This is very true, but no Dutchman goes to quite the length that the Chinaman does in the brilliancy of his hues and the daring of his conceptions. It is here that we notice his originality. There does not appear to be any rhyme or reason for his designs, and there is no precise rule that he follows. The result is always quaint, often grotesque, but invariably artistic. Gorgeous reds, yellows, blues and greens predominate, but somehow their flamboyant hues are never incongruous, but rather form a wonderful blaze of colour that charms the eye. It is purely Chinese, crude in a way but original and fascinating.

The Northern junks are not so fond of gay colours as are those of the South but even in Chefoo and other more Northern ports one will sometimes come across brilliantly decorated ships. Chiefly, however, the man of the North goes in for a plain coloured stern, possibly a bright blue or red, but in one colour only. The river type prefer the plain wood oil stain, well polished, and bright colours are eschewed. In some of the coasting types it is possible to tell from the colouring of a junk from which ports she hails, for each particular little village or port has its own special colour.

In the foregoing it has been the aim to convey to the reader the more interesting and important points in connection with native craft generally and it is to be hoped, therefore, that this introduction, together with the brief descriptions and sketches that follow, will enable those whose knowledge of Chinese vessels would willingly be enlarged to appreciate the beauty and efficiency of the Junk.

coasting types it is possible to tell from the colouring of a junk from which ports she hails, for each particular little village or port has its own special colour.

In the foregoing it has been the aim to convey to the reader the more interesting and important points in connection with native craft generally and it is to be hoped, therefore, that this introduction, together with the brief descriptions and sketches that follow, will enable those whose knowledge of Chinese vessels would willingly be enlarged to appreciate the beauty and efficiency of the junk.

THE
HOANGHO CH'UAN OR YELLOW RIVER JUNK.

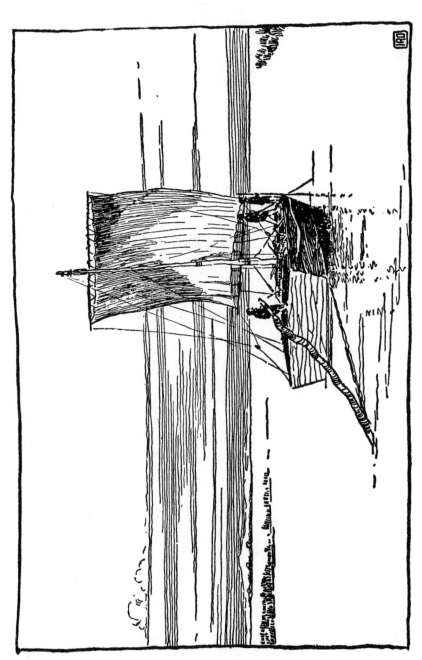

HOANGHO CH‘UAN

THE
HOANGHO CH'UAN OR YELLOW RIVER JUNK.

THIS extraordinary type of craft is to be found on the only navigable section of the upper regions of the Hoangho — China's second greatest river. They can hardly be described as boats or junks — floating packing cases would appear to be a more apt nomenclature.

They are built in a little village called Nan Haitze, four miles south of Paotowchen — a very important town fifteen miles from the borders of Shansi. A rather remarkable fact about these craft is that they seldom, if ever, make more than one trip. This is probably accounted for by their very fragile construction.

They trade between Paotow and Shetsuishan, (55 miles North-east of Ningsia), occasionally carrying imports on the upward journey, but more often going up empty and returning with wool and skins. They are usually tracked up on the voyage to Shetsuishan, taking nearly a month for the trip on account of the strong current met with there, while the return voyage takes only five days with the stream.

As mentioned above, these craft are so lightly built that one round trip is as much as they can stand, and on return to their home port they are invariably found useless for further service. They are then broken up and the remaining sound timbers are used in building a new boat.

Like the majority of Chinese craft the hull is of the open type, built of Tung Liu Mu and divided into three or more watertight(?) compartments. The planking throughout is not more than one inch thick and of very irregular shape. The whole fabric is held together by crude iron clamps while the general broadside appearance is very much like a jigsaw puzzle. The gaps left by the careless joinery are caulked with jute, hammered in with a chisel, no chennam or putty being used at all. The bow and stern are planked horizontally across with a rake inwards, while the bottom is flat, the boat drawing not more than a few inches fully loaded. Only a shallow draft vessel of this type could navigate successfully the shallows and flats of this particular section of the Yellow River.

The average size of a vessel of this type runs from 33 to 45 feet in length, the measurement of the one illustrated being approximately as follows:—

From bow to No. 1 bulkhead . . . 13 feet
„   No. 1 bulkhead to No. 2 . . . 16 „
„   No. 2   „   „ stern . . . 16 „

say   45 feet overall

The extreme breadth is about 20 feet while the depth measured from the top side of the bottom planking to the top of the bulwark amidships is six feet. The capacity of the vessel is 300 piculs (20 tons), the cargo being stored in the fore and aft compartments while the centre hold is covered over with matting when carrying passengers. A square lugsail of cotton cloth bent on a spar made of a "not very straight" tree trunk

THE HOANGHO CH'UAN OR YELLOW RIVER JUNK

with strengthening bits lashed on all the way up the mast
serves as a means of propulsion when winds are favourable,
while aft a sweep, some 40 feet in length, enables the Laopan
(Captain) to keep his boat straight.

with strengthening bits lashed on all the way up the mast,
serves as a means of propulsion when winds are favourable,
while aft a sweep, some 40 feet in length, enables the laopan
(Captain) to keep his boat straight.

THE TAKU FISHERMAN.

TAKU FISHERMAN

THE TAKU FISHERMAN.

THESE longshore fishermen never go far out to sea, but are to be found working close inshore off the edge of the innumerable sand and mud banks on the western shores of the Gulf of Pechili. On making the voyage from Tientsin to Shanghai by boat, one cannot fail to be impressed by the sight that meets one's eyes as the steamer, after passing the famous Taku Forts, makes her way through the Channel, past the Bar Lightship and out to sea. In the morning sunlight the misty horizon is broken up by white squares of light of varying, sizes, with an occasional red or brown patch. As the steamer approaches these patches of light take a more definite form, and will be found to be a large fleet of fishing boats hailing from Taku village making their way out to the fishing grounds on the Sha Liu Tien flats or off the southern coast of the Gulf of Pechili.

From 35 to 50 feet in length, they are of the flush decked type with a raised hatch combing of about 1 foot 6 inches high running amidships from abaft the foremast to what may be described as the break of the poop. There is considerable sheer fore and aft, the bow and stern being very bluff and of the box type. Both are about the same level as regards height from the water, while amidships there is little or no freeboard, the deck being awash at sea.

They are invariably two-masted craft, a very small foremast being stepped right forward of the hatch, while a heavy mainmast is stepped amidships. Occasionally a single big mainsail is set. This is assisted by a balloon jib set out on a boom over the bow taking the place of the foresail in other craft. The mainsail is of the usual straight leeched variety and is made of cotton cloth, the foresail or jib being of brown canvas or cloth. The crew's quarters are under deck, while aft a semi-circular mat house serves as protection for the helmsman.

The hull is built of soft wood, divided into compartments, but of very solid construction to stand the severe weather that is met with on the treacherous shallow gulf. In view of the waters in which these vessels work they are flat bottomed and of very shallow draft.

They have no colour with the exception of the occasional brown foresail, while a coating of wood oil serves as a protection against the weather.

THE PECHILI TRADER.

PECHILI TRADER

THE PECHILI TRADER.

T HE Pechili Trader is probably the oldest type of ocean-going Chinese junk. Representations of very similar craft will be found in the caves at Ajunta in India, and in the old temples at Boro Bodoer in Java. As late as 1903 these characteristically Chinese vessels were seen regularly in Singapore harbour. They are invariably large, running from 140 to 180 feet in length, by 20 to 30 feet beam, with a carrying capacity of some 4,000 to 6,000 piculs. The hull is of the "turret" build and sub-divided into watertight compartments. Although these vessels are built in Shanghai, their actual home port is Yingkow (Newchwang), while their trade routes are between Yingkow, Shanghai, and other Kiangsi and Chekiang ports. Curiously enough, however, they are owned and registered in Tungchow on the North Bank of the Yangtsze, some 50 miles north-west of Woosung, and their crews, which vary from 22 to 30 men, also hail from this port. Occasionally one will find a Laodah (Captain) from Ningpo.

These junks are always five-masted, and the peculiar method of stepping the masts is worthy of note. The foremast is placed right in the eyes outside the bulwark on the port side, the two mainmasts amidships, and in line (the after mast being the larger). The mizzen is just astern and in line with the rudder post. Just forward and to the port side of the rudder post, and clear of the tiller, another much smaller mizzen is fitted which is only used when going about or in light winds.

The reason given for this method of stepping the masts is that as these craft are very unwieldy, they require considerable sail area to drive them, which, for convenience in bringing the vessel into stays and paying her off in tacking, has been split up as much as possible. The sails have a straight leech and luff, and are lofty and narrow, with very little peak to the yard. A staysail is quite often set between the for'ard mainmast and the mainmast. This type is one of the very few Chinese junks carrying a topsail, but this is seldom used, and only when in very light air—a day of this kind being an occasion for making use of all kinds of sail quite unknown to the Westerner. To see a big craft of this type wallowing in the oily swell on a calm day, crowded with sail is an "eye-opener" to the methods employed by the Chinese sailorman to keep steerage way on his vessel.

Accommodation for the crew is provided in the roomy deck house aft, while a gallery extending some 10 or 12 feet out over the stern affords room for the navigator and the men handling the mizzen sails.

Beyond the carved railings and bulwarks there is no decoration except a little fretwork design on the lower side of the transom. The name and port of registry is written in Chinese characters set inside red circles on the stern quarters, and this is all the colour there is. One suit of wood oil per annum serves as a preservative.

The average time taken for a voyage from Newchwang to Shanghai is five days and nights provided there is a good breeze. Usually the voyage is direct to Shanghai, but if unfavourable winds are met with, Chefoo and Weihaiwei are taken in on the voyage.

THE YENTAI FISHER.

YENTAI FISHER.

THE YENTAI FISHER.

FISHING being one of the important industries of Chefoo, it is natural that the native fisherman has managed to design and build a boat singularly suited to his own particular calling. Of about 30 to 35 feet in length by 10 feet beam, her flush deck runs for'ard with very low freeboard amidships, rising in a sharp curve to the high bow on which a mooring cable spar and hand capstan are fitted. 20 feet from the stern a bulwark rising gradually from the deck to some 8 feet above the main deck at the stern forms a protection for the helmsman. The transom is open as is the case with most fishing craft in China, and a beam runs across joining the two stern wings. Below this and half the distance to the deck a windlass is fitted for hauling up the heavy rudder. This rudder is not fitted on pintles but runs through a couple of chocks on the stern post, one pair on a level with the main deck transom, while the other is some four feet lower down, thus enabling the rudder to be hauled up and down with ease, yet being held in position.

A hatch combing runs fore and aft ending in a raised hatchway through which entry is gained to the crew's accommodation under deck aft. In this respect she is similar to the Taku Fisherman, but has, however, very much more freeboard at the bow. The hull is sturdily built of soft wood and subdivided into the usual compartments which are used for the stowage of the catch. There are two masts on which the

Northern square leeched sails are bent, the foremast being canted well for'ard in the eyes of the ship, while the mainmast is stepped amidships. Occasionally two light vanes are fitted on either side of the transom which are only used for carrying the pennants.

THE YENTAI (CHEFOO) TRADER.

YENTAI (CHEFOO) TRADER

THE YENTAI (CHEFOO) TRADER.

IN searching round the water front in Chefoo harbour for types of interesting Chinese vessels, quite a number of the regular Chefoo Trader or Yentai Ch'uan, as they are known amongst the sea-faring people in this district, will be found. From outward appearances they are a poor craft, and of very little interest to the aesthetic taste of an artist. Similar as regards build, etc., to the "Antung Trader," which we might describe as the "mother" of all Shantung types, the cut of the stern, the splash of colour, and the joss paper placed on the transom proclaim the port from which she hails. Four masted, they run from 70 to 80 feet in length with a beam of 20 feet and are said to carry from 800 to 1,000 piculs. They trade chiefly between the ports on the Gulf of Pechili, and it is seldom that they are met with South of the north-east Promontory.

It will be interesting to note here that there are quite a number of sister types to the Yentai Ch'uan hailing from other important ports such as Lai Chow Fu and Yau Matau on the North coast of Shantung.

THE CHINCHOW TRADER.

CHINCHOW TRADER

THE CHINCHOW TRADER.

THIS is one of the few Northern types with any pretence of decoration, and is, as the illustration shows, very picturesque. Hailing from Chinchow fu (Fengtien), they are very seldom seen outside the Gulf of Pechili. They are about 80 to 90 feet in length by 18 to 19 feet beam and draw, when loaded, 7 feet with a capacity of approximately 400 piculs. Flush decked, with a high bulwark running fore and aft, the vessel has fairly high freeboard, which is somewhat unusual in these Northern types of craft. Invariably they are three masted, the foremast being stepped well for'ard at the break of the forecastle, and raking over the bows. The mainmast is amidships, while the mizzen — a very light pole — is found stepped right on the port quarter. On the low forecastle head, about a foot above the main deck, a heavy mooring spar is fitted which projects over the bluff bow. Through this the rope hawser is led and made fast to the hand windlasses on either side of the foremast tabernacle, and fitting into the bulwarks. Running aft from the foremast to the deck house a low hatchcombing, some 4 feet high by 6 feet in breadth, provides the necessary protection for the cargo stowed in the holds formed by the usual watertight compartments. Further windlasses on either side of the mainmast are used for heaving up the heavy mainsail, while aft in the cockpit over the well another one is fitted which is used for hauling up the rudder

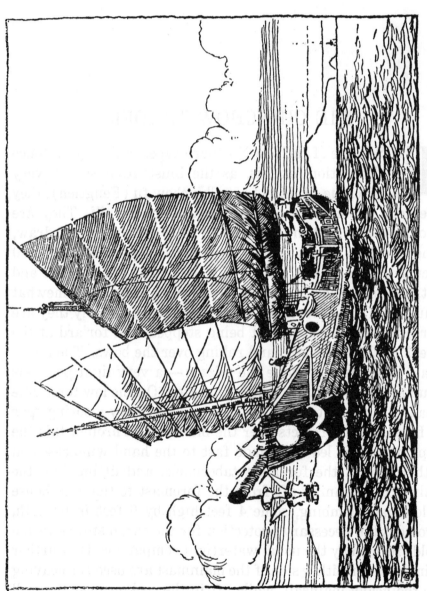

CHINCHOW TRADER OFF CHEFOO

when lying aground or at anchor. The vessel is navigated from the cockpit, the helmsman working the tiller by means of block and tackle. The stern is circular and somewhat unusual in design, as will be seen from the coloured illustration given.

Their regular route is Chinchow fu, Têngchow, Chefoo, Weihaiwei and Dalny, carrying cereals on the outward trip and Shantung produce on the homeward run.

It will be noticed that this Chinchow Trader has the Eye mentioned in my Introductory note.

These vessels are known as Hung T'ou Ch'uan (紅 頭 船) or " Red-headed Junks " !

THE ANTUNG TRADER.

ANTUNG TRADER

THE ANTUNG TRADER.

ANOTHER Northern type—flush decked, flat bottomed, and of shallow draught, 110 feet by 32 feet beam. She has considerable sheer from her high stern aft to the bluff box shaped bow, which rises abruptly from amidships where her freeboard is not more than a foot. Right over the bow, and extending some 4 or 5 feet, a heavy spar fitted on the end with a roller serves as a lead for the mooring tackle.

A raised hatch combing about 4 feet in height and of the same width runs from the foremast aft to the deck house, while for'ard there is a clear space of 10 or 12 feet where the windlass or capstan for hauling up the anchors or heavy sails is fitted. A clear space of about 6 feet between the transom and the after end of the deck house serves as a cockpit where the Laopan navigates the ship. The heavy rudder is fitted in sockets in a well, the head coming right through the cockpit, while the big tiller, extending well over the deck house is worked by a block and tackle made fast on either quarter.

These craft are usually four masted—two light pole mizzens being stepped on both quarters of the poop, while the heavy mainmast, fitted with sheaves at the truck through which the halliards run, is stepped amidships. The foremast is canted well over the bow. There are no bulwarks, and at sea the deck amidships is almost continually under water, the crew making their way fore and aft by the trunk amidships.

These junks vary in size from 50 to 250 tons, and are at the best slow moving and clumsy craft. The hull and masts are stained with a dark varnish, and beyond the little red diamond shaped joss papers stuck on the bow and stern wings, there is no other colour.

Their trade is from Antung to Shanghai which latter port with a fair wind they make in six or seven days. Sometimes owing to weather, Dairen, Chefoo and Weihaiwei are taken on the voyage. The chief cargo is oil in baskets.

THE SHITAU BAY TRADER.

SHITAU BAY TRADER

THE SHITAU BAY TRADER.

SOME of the handsomest junks that sail the China seas hail from the little village of Shitau, situated in the bay to the South-west of the South-east Promontory. They are square, bluff bowed, flush decked, and heavily built to stand the weather met with round this rock bound coast. A high bulwark extends from the deck house aft and ends in a sharp upward curve, forming wings with considerable flare on either side of the open bow. The usual hatch combing runs from the main deckhouse for'ard to the foremast, which is stepped well for'ard with considerable rake.

The deck house and crews' quarters are of solid construction, and extend from 10 to 15 feet aft of the mainmast, (stepped amidships), to the box-like stern. An open staging projects over the stern for 6 or 7 feet similar to that seen on the Pechili Trader. Of some 80 to 100 feet in length and 20 to 30 feet beam, the capacity of these junks varies from 70 to 250 tons and it is easy to distinguish them at sea by their bows and colouring. The flat square bowplate projecting out slightly on either side of the vessel is painted a bright red with a white circle in the centre on which the character "Fu" (府) is superimposed in black. The bow cheeks are green while a dark red varnish picked out with red facings forms the general scheme of decoration. Two prominent strakes (looking like single logs of wood) extending fore and aft are painted white, while up to the water lines the colour adopted is grey or black.

The big eye is placed in the usual position but somewhat lower down clear of the two white strakes.

Although there is a certain amount of trade between Shitau and Shanghai these junks invariably trade between Shantung ports and are seldom seen far away from home. Occasionally, however, one will be met with in the junk anchorage of the Native City at Shanghai.

THE LORCHA.

LORCHA.

THE LORCHA.

ON analysing the types of junks off the China coast for traces of occidental evolution, we find only one in which the slightest effect of this is noticeable. This is the "Lorcha" — a hybrid. The hull, although a type of its own has peculiarly western lines. The masts, three, are stepped in the usual Chinese manner, and the sails are of the ordinary Chinese lugsail type. This vessel only dates back a little before the Taiping Rebellion.

Originally built in 1843 by the Portuguese for repressing piracy, and also for convoying on the Canton Delta, they were often captured by the Pirates themselves. Also in a great many cases it was found that the Portuguese crews turned piratical. In 1847 seven Portuguese lorchas volunteered to sweep out the Pirates that infested the Ningpo waters, and after a bloody encounter accomplished their task. This is the last useful piece of work we read of them doing. As time went on the Portuguese owning these craft in Macao, finding convoys being no longer required, and no other profitable employment available for these vessels, they were sold, passing into various hands good and bad. In this way they drifted up the coast to Shanghai, Ningpo, and the River ports. It is said that by 1865 the Lorchas had practically disappeared from Macao waters.

During the above-mentioned Rebellion the Lorchas were bought by the adventurers that swarmed to Shanghai and the river ports in those days, and were used for gun running and all kinds of other contraband work. It is presumed, however, that in course of time they fell into reputable Chinese owners hands who found them a class of vessel very suitable for the Yangtsze trade.

They were built invariably at the Inner Praya at Macao — usually of teak and camphor wood. They were flat bottomed and of very light draft. The stern and rudder were of Chinese design and the craft well adapted for tacking.

The Lorcha unlike other native craft is always built with a straight keel that has no sheer fore and aft. The bowsprit which was undoubtedly made use of by the Portuguese for setting a forestay upon is still found on every vessel of this type but no use whatsoever is made of it; it would appear that the Chinaman using no stay finds this superfluous but nevertheless for "olo custom" has left it as it was. A relic of Western influence!

Another feature of this vessel is its colouring—the Lorcha is invariably painted a dirty red colour with a bright yellow poop and forecastle, while the prominent white deckhouses no doubt are responsible for the name by which she is known to the Chinese "Bai ao ch'iao" (白鰲壳) or "White Fish Shell."

It may be interesting to note that it was a Lorcha that was the immediate cause of the war between Great Britain and China in 1857–60 which has always been known as the "Arrow" war, after the name of the vessel in question.

THE TSUNGMING COTTON JUNK.

TSUNGMING COTTON JUNK

THE TSUNGMING COTTON JUNK.

THIS type, which will be familiar to everyone who has been up and down the Whangpu River, brings cotton and passengers from Tsungming Island at the mouth of the Yangtsze River to Shanghai. Of some 40 to 60 feet in length, with not more than 7 to 8 feet beam, they are flush decked with a small permanent house just aft of the mainmast which is stepped amidships. Fitted with leeboards, they usually have two or three masts, the mainmast being particularly lofty. To the average Westerner it would appear that these junks are over sparred and dangerous to a degree in a river such as the Whangpu where squalls are so frequent. To anyone who is observant, however, the reason for this high sail is obvious, for they are very fast boats even in a light wind, and never seem to miss any breeze over the banks of the river. The sail is of the ordinary straight leeched type fitted with innumerable battens, and in a squall the main halliard is let go, and down comes the sail with a crash. It is a sight to see two or three of these cotton junks when racing along in a strong wind suddenly drop their sails all together. This is the time to look for squalls for the Tungchow sailorman, through long experience on this run, has learnt the vicissitudes of the winds that are to be met with, and is very seldom taken unawares.

The hull is built of light pine on the turret principle, and in general appearance is very similar to the five masted Pechili trader described previously.

On any day these junks can be seen making their way up the Whangpu piled high with bales of cotton. The illustration given shews a craft of this type in a calm making her return trip to Tsungming for a fresh cargo of the staple for which that port is famous.

THE HANGCHOW BAY FISHER.

HANGCHOW BAY TRADER

THE HANGCHOW BAY TYPES.

BETWEEN Woosung and the mouth of the Yangtsze a never ending procession of craft of all kinds is met with, of which the Hangchow Bay fishers and traders may be singled out on account of their exceptional scheme of decoration. On the square box-shaped bow is painted a grotesque or conventional face, the nose, eyes and mouth being raised or appliqued in brilliant reds and blues, while the "Pa-kua" (a very common Chinese form of charm or talisman) appears in the same bright colours on either side of the bow. On the stern quarters a highly embellished Phœnix flies from aft for'ard while the transom is decorated with various figures according to the taste of the Laopan.

Both traders and fishers are box-shaped with a swim headed bow and square transom stern, flush decked, with a high bulwark running the full length of the vessel. The hull is flat bottomed and divided into compartments. They are of very light draft and carry a large sail area for their size, but as can be imagined their best point of sailing is "before" the wind. These junks are always fitted with leeboards.

There is very little difference between the Fishing junk illustrated on page 64 and the Trader which is shown opposite, except that the former very seldom exceeds 60 feet in length and only carries two masts, while the latter run up to 100 feet have three masts and carry up to 3,000 piculs. The fishing boats hail from Chapoo on the northern shores of the Hang-

HANGCHOW BAY FISHER

chow Bay while their fishing grounds are about the shallow waters of the Yangtsze estuary, and their market the great emporium of Shanghai. The Traders invariably hail from the ports on the southern shores of the Bay and are generally known as "Shaohsing" junks (紹興) after the important port of that name some 15 miles up the Yung Ho in Chekiang province. These traders are chiefly engaged in the carrying of firewood charcoal and cotton from Chekiang ports to Shanghai.

The smaller type of trading craft hailing from Haining and Kanpu (the chief port in China in the T'ang dynasty and often mentioned by Marco Polo) can be distinguished from the other Hangchow Bay types by the absence of the face on the bow which is painted a plain red with facings of the same colour on either side while a "phœnix" eye takes the place of the Pa-kua.

None of these Hangchow Bay types have any solid deck structures and accommodation for the crew is found under deck aft while a coach roof of Canton mats and bamboo laths forms protection for the helmsman and crew in dirty weather.

CHUSAN ARCHIPELAGO TYPES.

CHUSAN ARCHIPELAGO FISHER

CHUSAN ARCHIPELAGO TYPES.

THE type of junk that I have taken for my illustration is probably more familiar to the readers of this book than any of the others, and the traveller coming to Shanghai for the first time cannot fail to be struck by the numbers of these craft met with on the way from the mouth of the Yangtsze to Woosung and up the Whangpu River. Here is a vessel whose characteristic sheer, gay colours on the bow and the very striking eye that seems to look at the oncoming steamer with a surprised look, brings home very forcibly the fact that this is China.

Hailing from Shanghai and various ports in the Chekiang province and the Chusan Archipelago, they are generally known as "Ningpo Junks" but actually Chusan Island was their original home. Nowadays the vessels in practically every case are owned by natives of Ningpo.

There are two kinds of junks that come under this heading —one is the fisher and the other is the trader, and having taken the former for the subject of my illustration I shall deal with this type first.

The Chusan Archipelago Fisher is a beautiful, fast and seaworthy craft, and is typical of the type. Of 50 to 70 feet in length with a beam of 13 to 14 feet they have fine entrance, well cut-away forefoot and a "sweet" run, while the strong bulwarks running the full length of the ship gives a high freeboard and keeps the vessel dry. They are rigged with the usual China Lugsail and fitted with three masts. As a deep sea trawler the Chusan Archipelago Fisher is unequalled.

It is said that there are some 20,000 people engaged in the fishing industry in the Chusan Archipelago, the greater number of whom are without doubt on this type of boat. Their fishing grounds are off the islands of the Yangtsze estuary and round about the Chusan group, the catch being brought to Shanghai or Ningpo for sale. In the past these fishing junks were family owned, worked and run by the father and his sons, but at the present time the majority are in the hands of Chinese companies, the privately-owned vessel finding it more or less impossible to compete with the larger concerns.

The trading junks in general appearance are very similar to the fishing craft, but vary considerably in size, the smallest types having a carrying capacity of only about 200 piculs while the larger run up to 2,000 piculs (120 tons). The rig is the same in the majority of cases but a number of the smaller boats favour a spritsail on the mainmast instead of the usual lug. They have no particular trade routes and as far north as Tsingtao and Foochow in the south one will come across these ubiquitous traders. From Shanghai to Hangchow Bay ports, to Ningpo and the Chusan Islands, up and down the coast, on the rivers, the Chusan Archipelago traders ply their calling in all weathers and testify to the stoutness of their build and adaptability for the particular trade in which they are engaged.

Although there is a distinct similarity in build and exterior appearance between the Foochow Pole Junk and the type under review they must not be confused. The former junk is much

CHUSAN ARCHIPELAGO TYPES

larger in size and the elaborate scheme of decoration on the stern is absent in the smaller Chusan type where plain reds or blues with other coloured facings find favour.

THE NINGPO TRADER.

NINGPO TRADER

THE NINGPO TRADER.

NINGPO in Chekiang, some twelve miles from the mouth of the Yung river, is one of the first places in which foreigners settled. As early as 1533 the Portuguese colony known as Liampo was in a flourishing condition. We can be certain, therefore, that Ningpo was an important place in olden days. Shanghai has since eclipsed this one-time busy mart, and the fine vessels that used to carry the tea and other produce for which this port was famous have now nearly disappeared. The majority of junks seen moored along-side the river bank at Ningpo at the present time are of the Chusan Island, Shaoshing, or Foochow pole type, but occasionally one will see a real old Ningpo junk moored down by the Native City. If lucky, one will be met with outside Chinhai at the mouth of the River, and the illustration given shows one of these lumbering traders passing Tiger Island on her journey north. Of the turret type and similar in a great many ways to her sister vessel, the Pechili Trader (see page 28) she is infinitely more picturesque and, gliding along in the light breeze, the blue stern with red facings reflected in the muddy waters, with the brown and yellow of her sails contrasting with the sky, she is indeed a beautiful sight. Running up to 100 feet in length and carrying from 100 to 150 tons these Ningpo junks trade chiefly with Shantung and the Liaotung peninsula taking Ningpo cloths, varnish, felt hats, and peas, bringing back bean oil, wheat, skins, etc.

WENCHOW FISHER.

WENCHOW TRADER

WENCHOW FISHER.

AMONGST the innumerable islets off the coast of Chekiang one will often come across a fleet of fishing junks
hailing from Wenchow. To the Western yachtsman this
type of Chinese fishing boat appears extraordinarily efficient.
This is not surprising when it is borne in mind that the seas
in which they work are probably the most treacherous off the
China coast.

From 30 to 60 feet in length, flush decked, they are very
narrow, with not more than 10 to 12 feet beam. A high bulwark runs the full length of the boat giving ample freeboard
in heavy weather. Their general appearance is very picturesque, the bulwarks being brought down from the high stern
with considerable sheer and rising for'ard in a semi-circular
curve upwards forming high wings on both sides of the bow.
Here the wings are joined by a transverse beam on which the
anchor windlass is fitted. The stem head, usually a very solid
affair, tapers out from the waterline, meeting the main deck
at the open bow. A hand windlass fitted either side of the
mainmast serves as power for handling the sails, and another
one over the open transom stern is used for hauling up the
rudder. A raised hatch combing runs fore and aft, the hull
being sub-divided into numerous watertight compartments
in which the "catch" is stowed. There is no deck house in the
smaller types, a matshed serving as protection to the helmsman

WENCHOW FISHER.

while the crews' quarters are under deck. The colouring is distinctive and varies very little from the trader illustrated in colour on page 78.

FUKIEN TRADER FROM SANTUAO.

FUKIEN TRADER FROM SANTUAO.

FUKIEN TRADER FROM SANTUAO.

THE vessel illustrated here is of a type that is fast disappearing, and in fact is one that is very seldom seen nowadays. Hailing from Santuao in the Samsah Inlet —at one time a great tea shipping port — she is a very distinctive junk and has a somewhat Western appearance. There is a great similarity between this junk and the Foochow Pole Junk, Santuao and Foochow being very closely connected. The Santuao junk is, however, a much smaller type.

Varying in size from 60 to 70 feet in length by about 12 to 14 feet beam, they are usually three masted, the brown canvas sails being of the China Lugsail rig. The deck is flush fore and aft, the hatches being raised slightly above the level of the main deck, while a high bulwark runs the complete length of the ship and keeps the vessel dry. The hull is built of soft pine and is divided into watertight compartments. The forward lines are fine, while the " run " is carried out to the full beam, practically to the transom stern. The bow is of the open type, the bulwarks being carried forward and sheering upwards on either side and forming graceful "cheeks" with considerable flare. The big wooden and iron anchor, so common on Chinese coasting vessels will be seen stowed over the open bow. This is worked by a modern hand capstan fitted just forward of the foremast. A hand windlass between the mainmast and the bulwarks serves for power when "making sail" while two "horses," one forward of the mainmast, and the other aft are used for stowing the heavy yard and sails.

Quarters for the crew are provided in the deck house aft, while astern of the cabin bulkhead, where the heavy rudder head is brought up through the deck, an enclosed cockpit forms protection for the helmsman and navigator.

FOOCHOW LONGSHORE FISHER.

FOOCHOW LONGSHORE FISHER.

FOOCHOW LONGSHORE FISHERS.

OFF the mouth of the river Min where half a century ago the famous tea clippers dropped their pilots, cast off their tugs, and started on their long race for London, one will come across hundreds of small fishing craft hailing from Foochow and the quaint little towns and villages on the banks of this beautiful river. Amidst the beauty of the setting one can conjure up the picture sixty years ago — the blue dancing sea, dotted with junks, their brown sails showing up clear and picturesque contrasting with the graceful clippers, their royals and to' gallants'ls reaching up far into the sky, and shewing a dazzling white design against the green of the hills and the deep azure.

The Clippers have come and gone, but the Foochow Longshore Fishing Junk is still to be seen, and the illustration given shews a fleet of these on a calm hot day, after a storm, their brown mat sails, some torn to shreds, others full of holes, reflecting their colour on the still waters, and making a picture that one yearns to be able to do justice to.

These little seaboats, 30 feet in length, two and sometimes three masted, are flush decked and built with very sweet underwater lines, a fine bow and well cut away forefoot. As can be imagined they beat well to windward. There is no deck house, a matshed aft serving as protection for the helmsman, while the crew, of not more than four or five sailors, make shift for themselves under the deck aft.

The Foochow Longshore Fisher is a very good little sea boat, and even during the typhoon season one will see numbers of these small fishing craft miles out to sea scudding along before the wind.

FOOCHOW DEEP SEA FISHER.

FOOCHOW DEEP SEA FISHER.

FOOCHOW DEEP SEA FISHER.

HERE we see a boat that is akin to the Western trawler or drifter. Working out in the open seas in pairs they are sturdy vessels and can stand almost any weather. Considerably larger than the Longshore fisher just described, they are flush decked, with a high bulwark running the full length of the boat, giving them good freeboard and keeping them fairly clear of the water in heavy weather.

Off Matsu during the typhoon season these deep sea fishing craft may be seen running in under two or three reefs for shelter behind the islands, and I think the adverse critic of a Chinese junk would be inclined to change his views after seeing the behaviour of these junks in bad weather. In general appearance they would seem to be a "slow and unwieldy craft" as some writers take pleasure in describing them, and although the Chinaman has been conservative in his shipbuilding, he has like the Dutchman found little in modern practice to improve his vessel for the particular work for which it is built, and the Foochow Deep Sea Fisher is a case in point.

FOOCHOW POLE JUNK.

FOOCHOW POLE JUNK MAKING SAIL OFF WOOSUNG.

FOOCHOW POLE JUNK.

(*see Frontispiece*)

THIS type of junk, probably the most familiar to my readers is so named on account of the trade in which they are engaged, the carrying of poles from Foochow up and down the coast. They are invariably large vessels as far as Chinese coasting craft goes, and it is a common sight to meet one of these lumbering vessels while on a voyage up or down the coast of China.

Varying from 120 to 180 feet overall, with a beam of from 22 to 28 feet, they range in capacity from 3,000 up to 6,000 piculs (say 180 to 400 tons). The hull is of ordinary soft wood with hardwood frames and knees, and is divided into watertight compartments, the arrangement usually being sub-divided into transverse bulkheads every eight feet, and longitudinal bulkheads every four feet. This system of watertight compartments, besides being for the protection of the ship in case of accidents, has its commercial uses for it is the habit of the Chinese shipper to book one or more compartments at so much a voyage, into which he will cram as much freight as possible instead of the more common practice of Western shippers of booking so many tons of space at a given rate of freight. The deck is flush fore and aft, and a solid deck house rises high in the stern and forms a poop as in the galleons of Columbus's day.

Being specially built for their particular trade these junks have considerable tumble home amidships and aft, which facilitates the loading of the heavy cargo of poles stacked horizontally fore and aft, vertical cross pieces being fitted at regular intervals, and the whole being made fast by heavy bamboo hawsers passed right under the ship. Forward a fine entrance and flare will be noticed. There is no keel and the bottom of the hull has a marked flat surface which enables the vessel to lie safely aground without heeling over — a very necessary feature when one considers the numerous sandbanks these craft encounter on their voyages between Foochow, Shanghai and the lower Yangtsze ports. The water lines are carried out to their full beam practically right up to the transom, and one would imagine that although this gives the vessel great stability and greater ease in driving in a heavy following sea, it would also give her a tendency to pitch to a dangerous degree. Curiously enough this does not seem to be the case.

The transom is planked across for about half the depth to the waterline, where a well or trunk in which a large square rudder, very often weighing tons, is hung. At sea this rudder is lowered down the trunk and extends well beneath the ship. This together with the sharp forefoot helps considerably to hold the vessel up to the wind.

Not the least characteristic feature of the Foochow Pole Junk is the bow, which is peculiar to this type only. It is open at the top of the square stem piece on a level with the main deck while on either side are two wings which rise, curving to a sharp point and sheering aft towards the poop, and forming a fairly substantial bulwark and acting as a protection against the heavy seas likely to be met with. The stem head is invariably a solid piece of wood covered with an iron plate.

On this plate will more often than not be seen a familiar home advertisement, such as "Fry's Cocoa" or "Colman's Mustard." This curious feature is explained by the fact that a considerable quantity of old iron is imported into China from the United Kingdom, amongst which will be found some of the large iron-enamelled advertisements to be seen on the hoardings and at railway stations in England.

The masts, three in number, are invariably of iron-wood, the foremast having a striking rake forward being stepped well in the "eyes" of the ship. The mainmast, a massive pole is amidships and the mizzen, quite a light spar, will be found right on the after end of the high poop and slightly off the centre line for convenience when in "stays."

The sails are of the usual balance lug type, extended and stiffened by battens, and made of stiff white or brown canvas. The matting used in former days had given way to the modern and more convenient cloth.

In comparison with the Northern types of junks the afterleech of the sails has a distinct rounded shoulder while the luff runs straight up and down the mast. The Chinese sailorman uses no jib, and as he has his foremast raking well over the bow, the forward leech of his fores'l is extended well out before the mast bringing the centre of effort much further forward. Very often in light winds, however, one will come across a pole junk with a main staysail set between the fore and mainmast, and a flying topmast staysail aloft. Stunsails are also occasionally carried together with other strange sails that only a Chinese would think of using.

The decoration of a pole junk varies according to its home port, each particular village and sea port having its own distinctive colours. The elliptical transom stern affords the artistic shipbuilder an opportunity of displaying his originality and to those who are this way inclined I recommend the study of the stern of a pole junk. Nothing is too fantastic and although at times the designs are somewhat crude they are always original and fascinating.

The crew varying from 25 to 35 are housed in the deck house aft where ample and, according to Chinese standards, comfortable accommodation is found. The seafarers "Joss" (or God) is set up in this cabin and is the object of much "chin chinning" before the vessel proceeds on a voyage.

It is interesting to note here that the three most important oversea voyages made by Chinese craft in modern times have been undertaken by junks of this type:—

"Keying"   .   .   Hongkong to London, 1848.
"Whangho" .   .   Hongkong to Sydney, 1908.
"Ningpo"   .   .   Shanghai to San Francisco, 1912.

FOKIEN TRADER FROM CH'UAN CHOW.

FOKIEN TRADER FROM CH'UAN CHOW.

THE
FOKIEN TRADER FROM CH'UAN CHOW.

AT the mouth of the Chin Kiang river some 68 miles north-east of Amoy lies the city of Ch'uan Chow, very often called Chin Chew, and generally regarded as the Zaytun of Marco Polo's day. From this one-time prosperous port hails the type of junk here illustrated, and as regards build and decoration they are in my opinion the most beautiful boats on the China coast. Trading between Ch'uan Chow and Fukien ports to Shanghai and other places in the north, these "Pai ti ch'uan" (白底船) or white bottomed boats as they are called by the natives, are wonderful sea boats and yield nothing in the manner of handiness to any of our modern western sailing craft. Of not more than 75 feet in length by about 15 feet beam on deck, they have very fine bow lines and sharp entrance, while the "run" aft is very "sweet." There is, however, considerable tumble home amidships.

Although they have no keel, the rudder when at sea is lowered down and extends well beneath the ship, helping considerably to hold the vessel up to windward. Like the majority of South China craft, the stern is of the transom type, elliptical in shape, the stern wings or cheeks being extended slightly aft of the transom. The transom is planked horizontally for about half the distance from the top of the poop to the water line where a well is cut and the rudder fitted in sockets. This heavy piece of gear is handled by a windlass fitted between two bumpkins extending over the stern.

To see one of these Ch'uan Chow traders beating to wind-ward is a sight that will appeal to any sailor, while the colour which has been shewn in heraldic hatching in the accompany-ing pen and ink sketch will give the artist an idea of her picturesqueness.

AMOY FISHING JUNK.

AMOY FISHING JUNKS.

AMOY FISHING JUNK.

THIS type of fishing junk has probably the worst weather on the China coast to contend with, so it is not surprising that the Amoy fisherman has managed to build an exceptionally fast and sturdy craft. The Amoy fishing junk is now known to the world at large for only in 1922 a Capt. Waard took a vessel of this type across the Pacific to Vancouver thus proving the sea qualities of this Chinese boat. Of about 70 feet overall and 45 feet on the water line, the Amoy fishing junk has a beam of 18 to 19 feet and a moulded depth of 5 feet. Yacht measurement about 25 tons. Flush decks with no bulwarks there is considerable sheer both at the bow and stern, the sharp stem broadening out above the water line to the gunwale while the stern is of the transom type like the "Ch'uan Chow" trader, but open above the deck level. The vessel is steered by the long tiller of the heavy rudder fitted in sockets, on the transom, handled by the usual hand windlass between the stern cheeks.

A distinctive feature in these junks is that a high sail with straight leech and luff and 15 to 20 bamboo battens is favoured. This is the only vessel south of the Yangtsze cape which uses this type of sail. They are usually two masted craft, but very often a mizzen is stepped right on the starboard rail.

Off Quemoy, Taitan and Chapel Island one will come across this sturdy type of fishing craft in all kinds of weather and it is quite apparent that the builders knew their work. The long overhang only recently evolved by modern yacht constructors is another of those points which we can see from the build of the Amoy fishing junk was well understood by the Chinese shipbuilder from the very earliest days.

The decoration of a boat of this type is simple but attractive, the upper part of the flat bow piece being painted black with a white "Yin and Yang" circle, while the lower is red, the two being divided by two halves of an inverted crescent meeting in the centre. Up to the sheerstrake the bottom of the hull is painted white while topside a red varnish serves as a protection from the elements.

FOKIEN TRADER FROM AMOY.

FOKIEN TRADER FROM AMOY.

FOKIEN TRADER FROM AMOY.

IN the days of the early Arab traders Ch'uan Chow was the great shipping centre for Fokien province and it was from that port Kublai Khan despatched his expeditions to Java and Japan in the 11th century. In the past decade, however, this one-time famous port has been superseded by Amoy. Here the big trading junks hailing from Changchow, some 30 miles west of Amoy on the Sei Koe River, may be seen.

Not many years ago the forest of masts in the junk anchorage in the eastern quarter of the port of Amoy told one of a big trade in sailing craft, but as it is the whole world over, sail is gradually giving place to steam and the numbers of junks decrease noticeably year by year. The scene there is now rapidly losing its picturesqueness for the gay colouring of the junks and their sails is being replaced by the sombre black of the small coasting steamer's hull and the unkempt and dirty appearance of the innumerable steam launches that ply between the small ports up and down the coast and on the river.

The Amoy trader—as I shall call these junks (for undoubtedly their main port is Amoy, although Changchow may be their home)—are a type very slightly removed from the Fukien traders hailing from Foochow. To the average person the outward appearance is the same and it is only from the colour scheme that we can tell the port from which she hails. The bow in both types is the same but the colouring of the stem piece is an indication of the junk's native port, the Foochow type being painted red while the Amoy trader has the same decoration as the fishing junk from the same port and the trader from Ch'uan Chow. The stern in all the Fukien types is very similar but occasionally one will find a junk master from this province who has eschewed the gaudy figures of birds and dragons so often found on the other types from this part of China's seaboard and painted his transom some plain colour.

A junk of this kind runs up to 150 tons capacity and they trade between Amoy, Formosa, Shanghai and the southern China coast ports, often taking in Hainan and French Indo-China ports.

TRADER FROM CH'AO-CHOU.

TRADER FROM CH'AO-CHOU.

TRADER FROM CH'AO-CHOU.

C H'AO-CHOU FU, 25.5 miles from Swatow on the Han river, is the second city in Kwangtung province and as such is of no mean importance. As a port, however, its days are numbered for Swatow has taken away the one time important shipping trade. There still exists a number of large junks hailing from this place and quite often now one will come across a Ch'ao-chou trader off the coast of Kwangtung making her way slowly southwards or ratching up against the N.E. monsoon. In days gone by these vessels had a good trade with Siam, Hainan and the southern Kwangtung ports from which places they took cargoes to Shanghai and the north, but steamships have killed their trade and every year their number diminishes. Their routes are now practically confined to Pakhoi and ports on Hainan Island.

It is interesting to note here that in the early days these junks were invariably built in Siam, their crews were Ch'ao chou men, while they were owned by Chinese settlers in Siam or by Siamese nobles. Nowadays very few of them trade as far away as Siam, and Ch'ao-chou fu has become their home port.

These Ch'ao-chou junks are usually large craft, some running up to 250 and 300 tons capacity. In build they are a large type of Swatow fishing craft with the addition of a solid deck house aft and an enclosed elliptical stern. A section of the for'ard topside planking is painted a bright red with the usual eye, the general colour scheme of the hull being varnish with the lower strakes painted white. These vessels are known as "pak tow sun" (or Pai t'ou ch'uan) or "White Headed" junks.

. . . . .

My readers will no doubt have noticed from the sketches of types already given that in arranging this book I have worked from North to South, and it will be seen that the more southward we get the Chinese lugsail in use on the junks off the coast takes on a rounder shoulder to the leech culminating in the Hongkong types, where this is a particularly noticeable feature. In the Ch'ao-chou trader a compromise of the northern and southern types has been made use of, the foresail is of the northern straight leeched variety while the mainsail and mizzen follow the usual Hongkong fashion.

SWATOW FISHING BOATS.

SWATOW LONGSHORE FISHERS COMING TO THEIR ANCHORAGE

SWATOW FISHING BOATS.

SWATOW has a big trade in exports of dried and salted fish and it is said that the waters around this section of the coast are the finest fishing grounds on the China seas, Between Sugarloaf Island at the entrance to Swatow Harbour and the Lamocks, a group of rocky islets some 45 miles out to sea to the eastward, one will come across fleets of fishing craft of all sizes at work. Trawls down and reefed to the strong breeze they make a fascinating study as they roll to the freshening seas. The trim little craft that we see illustrated here hail from Swatow and the other towns and villages at the mouth of the Han River.

From 30 to 40 feet in length by about 8 to 10 feet beam these Swatow fishing junks have very fine lines fore and aft but are quite beamy amidships. The bow tapers up from the water line to a T-shaped stem head while the stern is of the usual open transom type. Usually two masted craft a very light mizzen is often carried while on occasions a single masted junk will be met with. The sail has a more rounded leech than the northern types of fishing vessels and is made of brown canvas or cloth stiffened by more than the usual number of bamboo battens, each with its own single part leading down to the main sheet. The scheme of decoration is simple, the hull being stained a dark brown with the usual native varnish while for'ard a couple of wales are painted a bright red on which the "oculus" is placed in order that the vessel may see her way.

To the traveller on a coasting steamer who is bored by an extra long stay in this port I can heartily recommend the study of these interesting boats as they pass to and fro. In the late afternoon or evening they return from their fishing grounds with the day's catch, and the scene is a lively and thrilling one. We first see them in the distance coming in together past Masu or Double Island as it is sometimes called, racing in to be the first with their catch on the market and as they near the Custom house several small sampans put out to meet them, each junk apparently having its own attendant. As the first vessel comes up at fairly high speed the foremost rower in the sampan drops his oar, throws a line to the larger boat to which it is promptly made fast. This is not done without a certain amount of risk as the sudden jerk, when the slack of the rope is taken up, throws everyone in the sampan off his feet. The first shock being over the sampan is drawn alongside and it is the work of but a few seconds to drop in the baskets of fish — the painter is then cast off again and the rowers take to their oars and race to the shore with the cheerful "chantie" of the stalwart oarsmen. 'Tis a smart piece of work, the whole operation occupying only a few minutes, and is an example of what small boats can do when skilfully handled. Here is also proof that the Chinese sailor is a master of his art.

HONGKONG FISHER.

HONGKONG FISHER.

HONGKONG FISHER.

IT would require the pen of a Kipling to do justice to the sight that meets the eye of the traveller aboard ship coming up the Lyemun pass in the early morning. Hundreds of junks large and small, all of the same type, will be seen beating out to sea, tacking in and out of the vendure clad islands, and making their way out to the fishing grounds off the "Ninepins" or "Waglan."

The Hongkong fishing junk or trawler is undoubtedly one of the handiest vessels in the world and more akin to Western ideas of a seaworthy boat, and although they have not the colour or picturesqueness of some of the northern types, they are nevertheless full of interest to the yachtsman. The hull in the Hongkong and southern types differs from the northern in several ways. The bow is sharp and has not the same upward sheer always seen up north. The deck-lines are comparatively level up to amidships where they are carried up sharply to the high stern galleries. In the bigger type of sea-going junk the "run" is brought in to a well rounded stern where the heavy rudder is shipped in sockets and hung by a tackle so that it can be adjusted for depth or raised completely when the vessel is beached. The underwater body of these junks is very sweet while the forefoot or gripe is extended well under the bow and assists in holding the vessel when beating to windward. The rudder is let down at sea and is used very much in the same way as we use a centreboard. A gallery is built well out over the bows of the boat and used for stowing and working the anchor while a staging extending some six feet over the stern adds greatly to the comfort and safety of the steersman and the men handling the mainsail.

The rake of the masts and the well rounded shoulder of the leech of the sail are distinctions by which one can easily distinguish this type of junk at sea. The sails have not the same number of battens as that of the northern types but the same rigging is in use. It will be noticed that the luff of the foresail is cut so as to stand out well before the mast, bringing the centre of effort much further forward than in any other type on the China coast. Invariably two masted craft, a mizzen is very often stepped right on one quarter of the poop and only set when the trawl is down and the mainsail not in use.

The trawlers operating off the coast of Hainan are similar in many respects to these Hongkong fishing junks.

HONGKONG TRADER.

HONGKONG TRADER

HONGKONG TRADER.

THIS type of native cargo carrier, like many other Chinese craft, is fast disappearing from the coastwise and river services. Brigandage and piracy on the Pearl (or West) river delta have driven them almost completely out of the trade, and nowadays they are more or less confined to the short overseas voyages to Hainan, Pakhoi, Kwangchow, and Indo-China ports.

To the traveller who is interested in shipping and craft, and yet who has not the time to make an extended trip up the coast, or in the interior, Hongkong is an ideal spot in which to study the Chinese craft close at hand. Here moored alongside the Praya, riding at anchor in the harbour off Wanchai, Shaukiwan or Aberdeen, large numbers of junks can be seen. These stout and sea-keeping vessels are worthy of close inspection, and are full of interest to the appreciative eye. An hour or two amongst Hongkong's native shipping would not be misspent and would convince even the most sceptical of the efficiency of the Chinese junk for the particular work for which they are built.

In build and general appearance the trader is in many respects the counterpart of its sister vessel the trawler, but of course the cargo type runs to much bigger tonnage. The average size of the type of coaster illustrated here is 120 tons although some may run up to 200 tons. They are mostly two masted craft — a small foremast is stepped well forward while the big main mast is amidships, both having a very characteristic cant towards the bow. Occasionally, however, a three masted junk will be met with.

Although the Hongkong fishing junk and the majority of traders do not affect any decoration at all, and are content with the plain dark red varnish, there are a number on which the captain or owner has let his artistic taste loose. The stern galleries are picked out in bright reds, yellows and greens, with perhaps a couple of crossed flags on the counter.

A feature worth noticing on a Hongkong junk is the perforation of the rudder with a number of diamond shaped holes. It is a general idea that this is common practice with Chinese craft, but in the majority of vessels north of Hongkong, this does not appear. There is no reason given for this practice, and the only explanation that is offered in reply to an enquiry is " to let the water through, of course."

The Hakka sailorman who is born and brought up on the water is probably one of the finest deep water sailors in the world. When one considers the variable weather he has to contend with, calms and sudden typhoons in summer, heavy squalls in winter that seem to spring out of a clear blue sky, it is little wonder that he has managed to evolve what is undoubtedly one of the handiest types of sailing craft in existence.

It is an interesting sight to watch a fleet of these vessels getting under way just after the Hongkong typhoon gun has gone off, and making for the typhoon shelters at Yaumati or Causeway bay. Excitement runs high, language is free, and collisions appear imminent, but the smoothness and precision with which the junkmaster works his junk through the crowded shipping speaks a lot for his skill and the handiness of his rig.

A word of warning, however — the cargo of a Hongkong trader is very often composed of sun-dried fish of an odour that the nose of the Westerner is unaccustomed to.

WAI P'I KU CH'UAN
OR ''CROOKED STERN BOAT.''

WAI P'I KU CH'UAN.

WAI P'I KU CH'UAN
OR "CROOKED STERN BOAT."

FROM Fu-chow in Szechuan there hails one of the most extraordinary vessels built, and no book on Chinese Water Craft would be complete without reference to this type of junk. It is found only on the Kung tan or Wu river at Fu-chow. This river is a very swift running one with a great many small rapids, making it difficult for an ordinary boat to navigate. A shallow draft boat with an ordinary rudder does not give enough steering power in this swirling water so that the boatman of the Kung-tan had to evolve some other means of managing his craft. In general arrangement the "Wai p'i ku" is very much the same as the other craft used on the large rivers, with the exception of the stern and steering arrangements, and that no sail is ever carried, the single mast being used for attaching the long tracking rope to.

Of about 50 to 70 feet in length, and 8 to 10 feet beam, and very shallow draft, they have no rudder at all, while the hull looks as though an ordinary river junk had met with an accident in which the stern had been badly twisted upwards on one side. The higher corner of the crooked stern supports an enormous sweep, very often 50 feet long, which is worked from a high crazy looking bridge built up over the deck house amidships. Another sweep, very much shorter, is fitted on a pivot aft on the starboard side at a point several feet below the main sweep. This is worked from the deck of the boat and is used in still water.

There are several theories put forward as to the reason for the design of these junks, the riverside boatmen arguing that as they always turn in one direction it was very necessary to build them in this manner so that they are enabled to pass by certain protruding rocks along the river in safety. Others state that it is on account of the superstition of the people who believe that these crooked sterns frustrate the powers of the evil spirits. In view of the high pivot required on which to work the big stern sweep I think that the builders were forced to construct the stern in this manner in order to get the necessary fulcrum for efficiency.

KAN CH'UAN.

KAN CH'UAN, KIANGSI.

KAN CH'UAN.

THE Kan Ch'uan, of from 30 to 40 tons capacity, 40 to 60 feet in length, by 6 or 7 feet beam, and of very shallow draft, is an interesting junk. She has practically no freeboard amidships when loaded, and her deck sheer rises sharply at the bow and stern. The hull is flat bottomed and built on the turret system, sub-divided into compartments, while the stem piece of heavy planking fitted athwartships, quadrant in form, curves up from the water line and forms an enclosed forecastle on top of which a couple of heavy "cat heads" are fitted for working the anchors. In the Kan Kiang or Kan river, there exist a number of bad rapids, and it is to prevent taking too much water aboard that the bows have been built up in this manner. The stern is similar in shape to the bow but rises somewhat higher.

A large balanced rudder is fitted under the stern, the rudder post being passed through a hole cut in the counter while the top of the blades is cut to fit the curved shape of the stern.

Just for'ard of the deck house, which is made of arched bamboo and covered with matting which extends from about 10 feet from the bow to the poop, is fitted the mainmast, while a mizzen is stepped right aft of the steering platform rising high in the stern.

The sail is of the usual balanced lug type with straight luff, the leech having a distinct rounded shoulder. It is interesting to note here that although the shape of the sail in these large river and lake types is similar to that of the sea-going craft, the sail is made in strips, the innumerable battens being laced in and out. What the reason for it is I am unable to ascertain.

The Kan Ch'uan trades from Kanchow-fu on the Kan Kiang to Kiukiang bringing down tea, camphor, grass cloth, beans, and taking back foreign imports from the important river ports.

CONCLUSION.

CONCLUSION.

THERE is a long oily swell. The sea is shimmering in the sunlight, while the little round copper coloured clouds, precursors of a typhoon, seem to hurry across the green sky as if bent upon some nefarious work. The Lammocks, where many a good ship has piled herself up in a typhoon, seem to wink at one. The brown rocks and bright green slopes topped by the black lighthouse on the southernmost islet indicate to the passenger that the journey is near its end, for Hongkong is the southern limit of our voyage in search of " Junk " types. We have travelled up the far reaches of the Hoang-ho; we have tapped the upper tributaries of the Yangtsze, and traversed the entire coast of China, but have only seen a very small fraction of the millions of craft that ply on the coast, rivers and lakes of China. We have, however, seen a variety of vessels that for beauty of line, decoration and general utility, have no counterpart in the world. The coloured illustrations will have shewn the reader the bright colours a Chinese sailor affects, but it must not be forgotten that only when newly-painted, can the colours be seen as shewn on the plates. It would probably take the uninitiated some time to recognise the types; time and the elements have helped to put a drab wash over the picture, and at their anchorage Chinese Junks appear sorry looking craft—nevertheless the beauty is there.

CHINESE JUNKS AND OTHER NATIVE CRAFT

It is, however, for the reader himself to look for them at sea, on the rivers, and in the interior on the lakes when he will understand how Chinese craft can exercise such fascination on the Western mind.

THE END

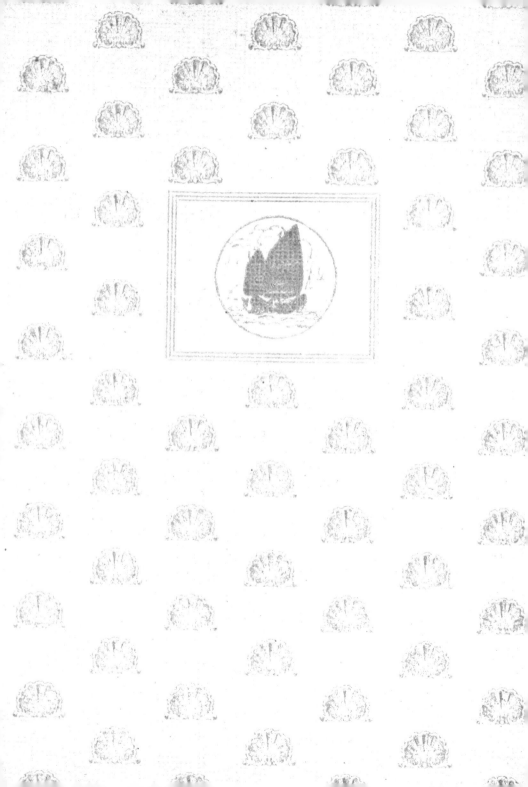